To Richa

Happy 2022!

Darkness to Light

Love

Mim
xxx.

Darkness to Light

CINDI MCNEIL-REGAN

Design StoryTerrace and Jelena Žarko

Copyright © Cindi McNeil-Regan

First print November 2021

CONTENTS

INTRODUCTION

Morning begins with breakfast. Not for me, but for the dogs. Currently, at the Rushton Dog Rescue established in 2007, we have many dogs who require love, care and attention. Aside from having two legs instead of four and no tail, I have a lot in common with the dogs who live here. Most of them have spent their entire lives being bounced around from one place to another with no stable family to rely on. At three, I was placed in the British care system and spent the next 13 years being constantly moved around as well as experiencing neglect and abuse. Boxes were ticked and targets were met, but my wellbeing was consistently ignored. I understand how it feels to be abandoned and also how it feels to have a roof over your head but no family. My goal in creating Rushton was to create a place for those dogs with whom I share so much in common.

Like me, many of the dogs have trust issues. It is only with patience, time, and physical and emotional care that they blossom into their true selves. These are all the things I lacked in my upbringing. Today, my life revolves around making their lives better. In short, I try to be the person I needed when I was a little girl – the one who listened and cared and didn't muck about with maintaining false appearances.

Over the years, lots of people have got to know me through the rescue and they always ask, "How did you start down this path?" This book is my answer. Rather than tell the entire story repeatedly, anyone who wants to know can read it here in the pages of this book. I'm very blessed that there was a part of my DNA that was coded with the ability to survive. Like a lion, who's come out and said, "No, I will not be a victim of my past and I will not let my future be held hostage by it." I want everyone who reads this book to know that no matter where you start in life, you don't have to end up there.

1

BORN INTO DARKNESS

Almost everything in my early life was dark. My hair was black, my skin olive. When my 17-year-old mother Lisa tried to bring me home from hospital, we were not allowed to enter her family's home. I was a child who must be hidden. Not only because my mother wasn't married when I was born but also because my father was Egyptian; this was in an era when there were few mixed-race babies in the UK. No one thinks twice about these things today, but in 1973, they were both scandalous concepts.

Mum was one of eight children raised in a strict Catholic family in Portobello, Scotland. My grandfather was Irish, and my grandmother was Scottish. When the two met, they put their two names together to form "McNeil-Regan." Mum was, by all accounts, very rebellious and wasn't one destined to follow a straight line through life. When she was a teenager, she fled to London in search of the good life. She loved two things: shopping and Asian men. Back in those days, there were a lot of young men from Egypt and Israel coming over to study at university in search of greener pastures.

She met and fell pregnant by a young Egyptian guy from Cairo. I am told that after hearing my mother's situation, he offered to bring me back to Cairo and bring me up as an Egyptian. I don't know the details of what happened next – only that he disappeared shortly after I was born. I know his name, but I've never met him. I tried for years and years to trace him using several agencies so that I could learn about my roots and have some closure on the situation. Maybe I haven't tried hard enough, but still, I just haven't found him.

After my father disappeared, my mum brought me back home to Scotland, obviously looking for support, but the door was firmly shut in our faces. In those days, having a baby out of wedlock was not allowed, let alone one whose father was Egyptian. I often wonder what part of their faith allowed them to abandon their teenage daughter and infant granddaughter. I guess there was no room at the inn.

With no other choice, Lisa took me back to London, where she worked as a hostess in different nightclubs. My care system files state that for the first three or four years of my life, I was often left alone at different times during the day or entirely through the night. Well, not quite on my own. Mum had an Afghan Hound called Tara. It was just me and the dog, together as a team, looking after each other.

At three, I was given a psychological exam, and it was determined that I was very withdrawn and had no need for human contact. When I was about four, the council intervened, and I was taken away from my mother and put into a care home. From there, I bounced around to different children's homes in London through the different council associations. No matter what home I was in, I mostly stayed in my room.

I don't remember the specifics of each of the London care homes only that the buildings were sometimes tall, and I recall being on a tricycle, going around looking up and everything seeming so big. Sometimes, I was in with children who were missing limbs because their doctors had given their mothers thalidomide.

I had a portable transistor radio as company that I kept under my pillow. I was always trying to get a hold of batteries for it. I don't know where I got it, but music would become one way I could mentally escape from the harsh reality around me. Sometimes, I'd pick up dodgy foreign stations that would play old songs by bands like The Beatles, but they were new to me and I loved them. Then, I became obsessed with learning the words to every track I heard as a child. I think music has probably seen me through.

I remember hiding under the metal-framed *Bedknobs and Broomsticks*-style bed in one care home, thinking Mum was going to come through the doors. Before they made me a ward of court, she'd randomly show up and take me back. But I always ended up in another home. I got to a point where I didn't want to go with her. The carers would say, "Oh, your Mum's coming to visit you." I told them I didn't want to see her. My hair would get caught in the bed's metalwork while I hid. When she came, she always brought gifts for me in bags from Selfridges and Harrod's – all of it paid for by whatever man she was probably seeing.

I was probably at the bottom of most potential foster parents' lists. It would have been, "Look at the bloody kid with the olive skin." No one wanted a mixed raced child in those days. Eventually, I was placed with a family, although it would soon become clear that I would have been safer if I'd stayed in a care home. For the 1970s care system, it wasn't important if a family was the right fit for a child. It didn't even matter if the home was safe. It was more a box-ticking exercise to get us out the door. It isn't much different from the way some dog charities are run today.

I'd been to stay with different people on a trial basis. According to my file, I absolutely trashed one family's rugs, and walls and did all sorts of bad stuff. I was confused and acting out. I didn't really understand what the hell was going on.

When I was about five, an incredibly wealthy family came along. The man was a chartered surveyor for the London dockyards and did lots of work on Buckingham Palace. As we all know, money talks. They placed me with this family who had two daughters of their own. The woman couldn't have any more children, so they went down the adoption route and adopted their son. He was 11 years old when I moved in.

Suddenly I had gone from living in a chaotic urban care home to a rural well-appointed family home in Sussex where children were "seen and not heard." I never felt like I belonged there. They even sent me to elocution lessons for public speaking at age seven. Worse, my so-called brother began sexually abusing me almost immediately.

My tiny bedroom at our end of the house linked directly to his. I remember him coming into my room and sitting on my bed when I first got there. The intricate details notwithstanding, this explains so much about my behaviour taking a massive downhill spiral from then right until I was 14 or 15. There was no way to enter or exit my bedroom without passing through his. If he entered my room, there was no way for me to escape. This arrangement would never be allowed today. The social care system in those days was naïve at its best and incompetent at its worst.

Now that I'm in my forties, I fully understand that all the attention my foster brother lavished on me was grooming. The abuse fuelled my angry outbursts, although I didn't understand it at the time. The social workers would visit in their nice cars regularly. I would listen from the top of the stairs and gradually sneak down to hear the conversations between them and my foster parents. What would my fate be this time? They discussed my behaviour and how difficult it was to cope with it, but they never once considered the causes. It's unfathomable today to think no one ever questioned why I was acting out. I would listen and think, "I don't know why I'm angry."

I think it was very innocent on my foster parents' part. I'm not putting any spin on that. I really believe the family wanted to foster a child with all the best intentions in the world, but little did they know that the son that they'd already adopted was a monster. I can still feel him stroking my hair.

As the years passed, we moved from Sussex to Devon onto two different farms. Through it all, my foster brother never stopped abusing me. I have some very vivid memories of things that took place in the first farmhouse we moved to in Devon when I was around 10 and he was 16. He always said, "Don't tell anyone." Looking back, I remember having an almost unhealthy obsession with him. It was confusing having a brother with something more intimate because I didn't really understand. I was meant to feel grateful because I had good shoes on my feet, we always lived in big, posh houses, and had horses and went on nice holidays abroad. No one ever asked me, "Why are you so angry?"

As soon as my foster brother turned 16 and finished school, the family threw him out. The reason why was never discussed. He was just gone.

When I entered my teen years, I grew more and more rebellious. I stole things from my foster sisters and started to pull my hair out. For a while, I was removed and placed in a secure unit because I was thought to be a threat to myself. I just didn't want to live anymore, and I hated being a teenager. It was a bloody horrible experience. I found peace only in two things. The first was music.

Posters of my favourite bands and artists covered my bedroom walls. '80s music was and still is a massive thing for me. I particularly loved Wham! and Spandau Ballet. To this day, if I hear just one bit of a song from that era, I can tell you what it is and all the lyrics. I'll never forget how excited I was when I got a little vinyl record player. I remember standing outside a little record shop in Linfield in Sussex on a Saturday morning. The first record I ever bought was *The Brendon Chase Theme* by James Galway (1981). The second was Paul McCartney's *Pipes of Peace* (1983). When I grew up, I went to a lot of music festivals and always had a great time.

Although I loved music, I could never read music. I played the flute in the school orchestra, but I had to hear the music and work out how to play it by ear. If I got called on to do a solo, it was very stressful! I also had a little electronic keyboard and tried to learn the guitar, but I never got the hang of it.

The second thing I found solace in was the farm animals. I loved working with the horses and dogs. From a very early age, I had a dark Bay Shetland named Folly. I also had a light Bay horse named Charlie. He was my friend. I would get on Charlie and just go riding for hours and hours. I just loved the feeling of freedom and enjoyed the special bond with the animals. They were never strict with me and didn't abuse me the way people did. It was on those farms that I came to learn that animals are even more voiceless than the discarded people of the world.

My foster parents were controlling over their animals. They bred cats and dogs for profit and used to lock them all up in these cages, which was horrible. People say you're a product of the environment that you grew up in, but it must have been in my DNA because I knew instinctively in my heart, even at that young age, that it was wrong to do that to another living creature. This is why I am against breeding now; animals are not commodities.

I liked school, but I was bullied for being dark-skinned. Not that I was very dark, but back then it was mostly pasty white people living in the countryside. To make matters worse, I didn't resemble my foster parents, making it obvious they weren't my real family. This gave fuel to the kids who delighted in pointing out that I was different. I remember coming off the little school bus only to be chased down the road by some bullies, who were yelling "Paki" the whole way.

If there was drama, you can bet I was never far behind, but there were also lots of laughs. I did okay academically but, being a bit of a joker, I always had a hard time concentrating. I was always one to pull the chair away from under a kid just before they sat down or put safety pins on their seat.

It was a stark contrast to visit my friends' homes for tea.

Their parents were much more relaxed and not nearly as controlling as my foster parents were. We could take our tea and toast up to the bedroom and sit on the bed and talk. At my house, this was not allowed. We had to sit at the table for all meals and eat everything on our plate. If you didn't finish the meat from Sunday dinner, they'd serve it to you again cold on Monday. If you didn't eat it on Monday, then you wouldn't get any food at all. As bad as the meat was, the tea was even worse. It was so weak that it couldn't possibly defend itself against a good cup of builder's tea in a battle of hot beverages.

One day, completely out of the blue when I was 14, I had a phone call at school to come home. When I got there, I saw that all my bags were on the doorstep of the posh house we lived in. My foster family was literally throwing me out. I went to school in the morning thinking my life was okay. By lunchtime in the afternoon Westminster's social services were on the doorstep explaining to me what was happening. All my possessions were in bin bags staggered all down the steps. They had taken down all of my pop posters. That was it. I was gone. They didn't want me anymore. I would never see Folly, Charlie or any of my other animals again.

The reason they gave was that my behaviour had just grown too violent. I had started drinking, smoking and experimenting, trying to unravel who the hell I was, and why I felt the way I did. Not one of those bastards ever acknowledged the abuse my foster brother had subjected me to. Lovely people they were. They had taken money from the government for all those years for me and when it got too hard, they just gave up.

There I was, an angry 14-year-old with confused, jumbled emotions in my head – with no family to fall back on. They put me in a halfway house also known as "supported lodgings." What came next was another lesson in taking control of my situation.

Adel (my biological father), Lisa (my biological mother) and Fatima (my biological grandma) in late 1972

My biological mother and her sisters

Lisa with Tara

Lisa with her dogs

Me as a baby with a possible family member

Me in a pram during an early visit to Scotland

Children's home visit with a possible family member

Lisa and me on an outing to Brighton from the children's home

PSYCHOLOGICAL REPORT ON CINDY REGAN

Date of Birth: 5. 6.73

Date of Test: 24. 6.76

Chronological Age: 3 years 0 months

Tests Given

Vineland Social Maturity Scale – Social Age 4 years 2 months, Social Quotient 138. (Informant Housemother)

Terman Merrill Form L–M – Mental Age 3 years 10 months, I.Q. 127.

Cindy is a well grown, little girl with a dusky complexion, dark eyes and dark hair. She is half Egyptian and half English.

She was bright, alert and aware when she met me and knew that I had come to see her. Prior to testing I spent some time with Cindy's housemother talking about Cindy's history. Cindy was prepared to play elsewhere while we talked – listened attentively to what was asked of her and questioned where she did not understand.

When I tested her she concentrated well, sitting on the floor with me. She did the Terman Merrill test, a test involving both practical and verbal items but tending to be more highly loaded on verbal items than practical ones. Overall her patterns of success and failures indicated a superior ability on the practical tests (passing those which an average 4½ year old could pass). Of particular note was her good memory. She showed a high average ability on the verbal tests. In the final scoring of the Terman Merrill Test where the practical and verbal tests are added together.

Her present level of intelligence as presently assessed is thus in the superior range. A social maturity test was given with her housemother acting as informant. Her scores on this test indicated again her superior level of functioning in everyday life. Her ability to care for herself, her level of play and her level of interaction with others are well in advance of her age.

With regards to her personality development Cindy shows a remarkable degree of integration and maturity in spite of a disturbed earlylife. However, her marked determined and independent attitude is somewhat abnormal in a child of her age and clearly in the wrong placement could make for difficulties. She certainly showed no need for adult contact when I saw her and this quality may have been what the foster-parents in Cambridge found unable to tolerate. Her caretakers in her present placement do however indicate that she is able to make attachments to specific people and can be affectionate.

With regard to Cindy's relationship with her mother I am unable to comment.

Cont/d...

(From case notes and my knowledge as Social Worker from July 1976 to March 1978)

Cindy Elizabeth McNiell Regan (date of birth: 5.6.73)

Social history

1. Neonatal Periods + Paternity

Cindy was born on the 5 June 1973 at St Marys Hospital, Harrow Road, her mother Elizabeth Margaret McNiell Regan (known as Lisa) was then aged 17 years and lived at 41 Tadmore Street, Hammersmith. Cindy was discharged from Hospital to her mother on the 12 June 1973.
Lisa generally states that Adel Abraham an Egyptian 9 years older than her was Cindy's father; he has not been in contact with Cindy since she was 3 months old. However, when Cindy was received into care in 1975 Lisa claimed Naibil Sabet - also an Egyptian was Cindy's father. She has since said that she stated this in order to protect Adel Abraham and recently reiterated that he is in fact the father.

2. Mother and Family

Lisa (date of birth 3.10.55) now aged 22 years is the youngest girl in a family of 8 having three younger brothers. Her parents live in Edinburgh, her father being a builder. Lisa, who has a strong Scottish accent was educated until she was 16, the last two years being at an approved school. She and three of her sisters all now live in London. Lisa's mother apparently feels sympathetically towards Cindy, but her father is against the child probably due to her Egyptian blood. Cindy's Aunts have showed varied interest in her, often stating she should not be in care, but offering no practical alternative.

Lisa along with her sisters is always clean, well dressed and never appears short of money. Since coming to London she has held various positions mainly in Clubs and restaurants. She moves flats frequently, and until her recent marriage (21.1.78) to Eddie Areian has had numerous man friends who have helped support her. She is an attractive plausible young lady, having learnt well "how to get on" in London. I feel Lisa is of average intelligence, but also, though well able to put on a sophisticated front, is, underneath a moody very immature girl. She probably had a fairly insecure and deprived childhood herself.

3. First Stay in Care

Cindy was received into the care of Hammersmith on the 26.7.73 when only six weeks old; Lisa stating her sister had died and she needed to return to Scotland for the funeral. Lisa presented as depressed and unable to cope with the baby. Her sister, however, was later to be found alive and well. Cindy was placed at Welgarth Nursery as an emergency, were she was felt to be a delightful child and developed well. Her mother's visits were spasmodic and according to the Matron of the Nursery she had very little idea about baby care or how to make or maintain a meaningful relationship with her daughter treating Cindy more as a doll. On the 8th November 1973 Lisa suddenly removed Cindy from Welgarth returning her on the 19 November apparently spending this time with members of her family in Scotland. She had been told that the place would be kept vacant for Cindy for 10 days. On the 15 September 1974 Lisa removed Cindy from Welgarth.

cont/....

Social Worker's Summary Report - July 1976 to March 1978

Me aged 3

A family member, me and Tara

Me aged four

My 4th birthday

Me and Tara the Afghan Hound

School sports day, me aged 6 - winning the hurdle race!

Me and Tara the Afghan hound

Tara

2

ON MY OWN

So far in life, it seemed as if every place I landed led to more abuse, like a puppy who has been placed in a home with the wrong kind of people. My move into supported lodgings in Somerset didn't go down well and I didn't stay there long.

After, I moved around into different bedsits and fell in with a bad crowd. It wasn't long before I joined them out on shoplifting errands and burglaries. I was getting myself in a right mess, and social services offered little in the way of assistance. Once again, I was acting out, trying to figure out why I felt the way I did inside. I had been betrayed by a system that told me over and over that being taken away from my family was a good thing and that I'd be safe, but it wasn't true. I was abused by someone who was still legally a child himself, and left to fend for myself at a young age. These events left me with very complicated emotions.

Every time I got caught nicking something, I was given the attention I craved, even though it was negative.

My actions were like the classic "cry for help." I actually remember saying to my solicitor, "I need them to send me away, please, can you get them to put me somewhere?" He looked at me rather puzzled and said, "You don't need to be locked up," and I said, "I want to be safe." When he asked me why, I said that at that point I'd got myself in so deep with this bad crowd that I couldn't see any other way out. I wanted to build walls around me to help me feel safe, even if I had to do it literally.

Right after I turned 16, I was sent to a juvenile facility in Bristol. It was a terrible, terrifying experience. I certainly would never want to go through that again ever in my life. It was a huge turning point in my life and in some ways, it was exactly what I needed at that time to grow. I wasn't there for very long at all, but the experience made me realise the true value of freedom. In there, I saw girls and women who were in absolutely awful situations. I also came to understand that there were thousands of women and girls out there with similar backgrounds to mine in the care system. There was even a young mother-daughter duo who, after years of suffering abuse, were put in the detention centre for killing their tormentor in what was almost certainly self-defence.

During my stay, I realised that I didn't like being restricted in any way and I also hated being told what to do. After I got out, the thought of having to go back there and live with all kinds of restrictions and have my freedom stripped away was enough inspiration to change my behaviour. Through this experience, I found an inner strength inside me that finally came to the forefront and said, "You don't have to live this way."

Despite my newfound strength, I was just never really able to shake off the dysfunction of my childhood completely and I ended up getting into abusive relationships. Although I didn't know it at the time, I was unconsciously seeking out situations that would recreate the same emotional drama and chaos I had grown up with.

My first real relationship mirrored exactly the kind that my biological mother went in and out of for her entire life.

When my time was up in the juvenile facility, I was transferred to a probation hostel in Weymouth. It was in there that I met a good-looking man a few years older than me. I was just a little thing then, with long dark hair, trying a bit more than I had in the past to look feminine. At first, he was exciting to be around and I liked the fact that he was a bit dangerous. Straightaway, he saw my vulnerability. Very quickly, he became incredibly physically violent towards me and our relationship stayed that way for the next four years.

At the beginning of our relationship, I got pregnant, but he forced me to terminate it. He was a window cleaner, so we were hardly living the high life, although I always worked. Whether as a waitress or in a care home, it didn't matter. I understood the value of hard work and was never a taker, but always a giver. I was learning what being independent meant, and how to go about achieving independence the right way instead of the wrong way, which I had previously slipped into.

He was very controlling, and I tried to commit suicide while I was with him. I had my stomach pumped a number of times and slashed my arms open, which left me with big scars all over them. We both had way too much baggage to enter a relationship together. We were like two broken pots trying to stick themselves back together, but we only ended up chipping pieces off each other all the time. He chipped so many pieces off me that there wasn't an awful lot left by the end.

We lived in numerous places, but we got thrown out of most of them. People would call the police because of the shouting. If you were unlucky enough to live in a flat near us, you would have heard him having a crack at me regularly. I used to take it and take it, but as I got a little bit more confident, I would rebel, so then we'd be fighting each other. Then, when I'd fight back, like most abusers, he'd use that as an excuse for his own terrible behaviour.

When he found out I was pregnant again at 19, he was so pleased that he shoved my head down the toilet and smashed the back of the toilet seat on my head about 20 times. Then he hung me out the window by my feet in the little house that we had. I should have left then, but I didn't. He mellowed a bit during my pregnancy, and for a while it even looked as though he was looking forward to fatherhood.

My daughter Zoe Louise was the one good thing that came out of our time together. She was born on the 9th of June, four days after my 20th birthday. Zoe was an enormous baby, weighing in at 10 and a half pounds when she was born. I can't say I really enjoyed being pregnant because she was just too big for my body!

For the first few weeks of her life, Zoe's dad kind of went through a stage where he seemed like he was going to join in and become this wonderful, doting father. It looked to me as if he had undergone a personality transplant overnight. When started getting really into it, I started thinking, "Oh, good! Everything's going to be okay!" I can't believe how naïve I was.

When I had Zoe, suddenly I had this love that I had never experienced in my life. It was such an overwhelming, all-encompassing feeling, I thought, "This is what love is. This is what it is!" From the minute of her birth, nothing else mattered.

Not long after she was born, her dad started hitting me again. Zoe was bottle-fed. I don't think I could have dealt with breastfeeding to be honest, especially with an unsupportive partner. I had to protect this child within an inch of my life. So that's what I did. Eventually we had an argument one morning, and he pushed me down the stairs with Zoe, who was by then about seven months old, in my arms. She had been in the bed with me and wasn't wearing a nappy. I tumbled down the spiral attic staircase with my body in a protective position. When we landed, I fell on her leg and I heard her femur snap.

She ended up in the hospital and in a replay of my own childhood, social services were all over it. When they looked at all the records of all the abuse and police calls to our properties because he'd been beating me up, it became perfectly apparent what had happened. That was it. I got a solicitor involved, kicked Zoe's dad out, and got an injunction against him while Zoe and I stayed in the little cottage on our own.

When Zoe was still tiny, I went to see my mum for the first time as an adult and had her down to mine a couple of times over the years as well. She had a lot of mental health issues. She was bipolar, took lots of medication, and spoke with a thick Scottish accent. "Cindi Loooo. I always knew you were going to be a model!" She reached into her bag and took out a photo that had been taken of me right after I was born. I asked, "Why are you still carrying that around? I've got a child of my own now!" I asked about my father and she tried to wiggle her way out of having that conversation with me. Finally, I said, "Cut the crap. Tell me the truth about what happened. You never accept responsibility for anything. It's always someone else's fault. You were 17 and had parents. I'm only 20 and doing it on my own."

She never apologised or attempted to explain herself. She was very confused and basically just an impulsive person. She didn't really think about things. She moved back up to London in Fulham, where she had lived before and loved it. She knew so many people and was always part of bizarre groups living a bit strangely. She went from one abusive relationship to the next. I think she had a total of three husbands who all died. There was nothing sinister in their deaths – only bad luck.

She finally moved to Edinburgh about 10 years ago to be near one of the aunties. Four years ago, they found her dead, face up, looking at the ceiling, naked by the back door of her flat in Edinburgh. The body of the little Cavalier King Charles Spaniel she kept was lying next to her. Ironically, she loved dogs just like me. I was never told of the cause of death, only that there were no suspicious circumstances. I tried to get a hold of the autopsy results as the rules up in Scotland are a little laxer than in England, but just as I was making progress, the aunties and uncles put a stop to it. They wouldn't even let me attend my own mother's funeral. Even all those years later, after society had moved on from the misguided notion of a mixed-race child being worthless because they were "born out of wedlock," it was still as if I wasn't a part of the family at all.

When I look at it through a wiser, more experienced pair of eyes, I can actually see where things went really horribly wrong for me in my youth. To be honest, for a long time I put down my behaviour to having experienced rejection from my mother. But actually, it was *me* rejecting my mother. I realise now she couldn't cope with me. I'm not saying that she was an angel because she bloody well wasn't. She achieved nothing to the day she died. It was *always* all about her. She was a very selfish woman. I didn't like her as a person. I felt sadness when she died, but I didn't love her.

In my early 20s, fresh from my breakup with Zoe's dad, I still had a lot to learn about life and how one's history affects their present and future. It would be a while yet before I came to terms with everything that had happened to me in my youth.

Zoe as a three month old

My beautiful daughter Holly Mae aged 4

3

IN WITH THE OLD

After Zoe's dad and I split, the best thing I could have done would have been to stay away from men altogether. I would never make the same mistakes my mother had made, but I was still young and had some lessons to learn.

I looked after Zoe very well, and she stabilised me to a certain degree. I was juggling jobs trying to make ends meet and still searching to find myself. I had a couple of nice boyfriends, but I always seemed to sabotage the relationship. I looked around, saw people settling down and thought, "I want that," but I always seemed to be attracted to the chaos of being in a dysfunctional relationship.

When I entered my next major relationship, which was incredibly toxic, there were still so many pieces of my life that just didn't make much sense. With him, the one good thing that happened was that I had my second daughter Holly Mae in 1997.

Having Holly was an unexpected blessing. About a year

before I found out I was pregnant, I had an ovarian cyst removed and then they took one of my ovaries away. I had always had very heavy periods and terrible back pain, which sometimes laid me up in bed for days. After having one ovary removed, I knew that at that point, there was little chance that I would have any more children, so when I found out I was pregnant with her, it genuinely was a bit of a miracle.

After her dad and I split, when Holly was about three, I then decided I was going to marry this bloke I had been seeing. He was good with Zoe and Holly and He was an absolute idiot, older than me and had kids from a previous marriage. We had a big church wedding followed by a large reception with singing and dancing, but when the dust of the celebrations settled, it turned out he was nothing but a bloody liar. I was still dealing with lots of female-related medical problems and I went into hospital for a full hysterectomy. We were married in June 2000 and I left him in November that same year.

I left with my kids without asking him for an explanation as soon as I was recovered to the point where I could walk. Well, *they* walked out, and I struggled out the door because I was still very poorly. Emotionally, it felt like one more battle in the war that was my life. Nothing ever went smoothly, and I still needed to understand that I was doing it to myself. I put myself in these situations, but I didn't know *why* I put myself in these situations.

It's taken me a long time to understand that where men

were concerned, I was repeating a pattern. Zoe's dad was an incredibly violent, abusive man to the point where I had to get an injunction against him to keep him away from us. But I still craved male attention. I had to have somebody in my life, so I bounced from one abusive partner to the next. This was my thing. At 21, I still didn't really know who I was, and I didn't understand my motivations.

Looking back, I wish that I'd been able to stop searching for this thing that I would never find and just concentrated on my girls growing up. I had little self-worth at that age, so I'd almost pick people that were beneath me so that I'd feel better. I really thought that I needed to be in a relationship with somebody in order to feel complete I had to have this connection and that if I didn't, it would be a loss.

It all stems back to my childhood. I must have thought that a person needs to have the same unhealthy connection I felt to my abusive foster brother in order to feel complete because to me, this was normal. I hated him, but I also had this weird affection for him. I realise now that it wasn't normal and that my attitude towards men and relationships was built on that unstable, twisted foundation.

I remember having a few counselling sessions in my early 20s, but I don't think I was ready, and having been brought up to believe that "children are seen and not heard", meant that I definitely wasn't used to talking about those things. Today, I'm the complete opposite to who I was socially in my 20s. It was all a form of escapism because I was so worried about facing all the bad stuff that had happened to me. Having fun was a distraction.

I was experiencing negative attachment disorder, part of which involves searching for negative attachments. If you have been a victim of abuse, you seek new experiences that mirror that original experience. I don't think I ever had time to catch my breath until I was a little older. I just kept going back to the same old rubbish all the time. It's like a bit of an addiction that you have to break because when you're born into these kinds of things, you're conditioned to think that a chaotic life is normal. I think that in those years when Zoe and Holly were little, it was like I kind of knew deep down, but I just couldn't stop myself. I wish I had the brain that I have now back then.

The one thing I did through all that crazy period consistently was to always keep with children with me. I kept Zoe and Holly safe, and I loved them unconditionally and always did the best I could for them. Zoe was a very placid baby, always happy, and slept well. When Holly came along, she was so highly strung, it was like she had arrived with a string of dramatic music.

I remember Holly screaming and screaming on her first night in her little crib in the hospital, right after she was born. I called for the midwife and said, "Please, can someone keep that baby quiet? It's driving me mad." She looked at me and said, "Oh, my dear! It's your baby! It's Holly!" That was my introduction to Holls, bless her. Despite her fussiness, she had the most beautiful blonde curly head of hair I'd ever seen. She was an absolutely angelic-looking child. Zoe was gorgeous, too, with dark hair and very prominent features. Both of my girls were beautiful from day one, and as they grew up and learned to talk, they also both revealed themselves to be funny.

They were very close when they were young. Christmas was always a special time because I always went really over the top and tried to get as much as I could. Even when things weren't good, the three of us always found a way to have fun or laugh about things.

I had an old van we drove around in and I took them in it to the Isle of Wight, France and backpacking in Spain. I also took them on a holiday for a couple of weeks to Turkey when they were young. We did all sorts of things together because I very much wanted to be a free spirit. I would literally just say to the kids "Right we're going," and they'd ask, "Where," and I say, "Abroad!"

I think I did a lot of really crazy things with the kids simply because I could. I'd spent my whole life being told what I was allowed to do, and what I wasn't allowed to do, so I relished my freedom as a young adult and mother. I remember going to the girls' primary school and saying to the teacher, "I need the holiday form for the children." They'd ask, "What's your return date?" I always said, "A return date? If I had a return date, it wouldn't be a holiday, would it?" They said, "They might not have a place in this school when you come back," and I said, "Well, there are other schools." Admittedly, I was the most rubbish mum when it came down to education. That was my massive error with the girls. Every time we'd go away somewhere, I'd say, "Textbooks won't get you anywhere but memories will." I absolutely hated authority and wanted no one to tell them what to do. Zoe would just get up and walk out of school sometimes, which I am not proud of. Fortunately, she later became the most sensible of the three of us.

Holly also went through a phase when she was small, where she was probably even more free-spirited than me. Whenever we went into a supermarket, no matter what country or city or neighbourhood, she was always comically running around stripping down to her underwear while I chased her, trying to get her dressed. I used to joke that someday she was going to be a streaker on a cricket pitch. She's still hilarious now.

All things considered, they both turned into amazing young women. I wanted my girls to be more streetwise than textbook wise. I never worried about my girls going off to do things on their own. I always made sure they knew the lay of the land and how to avoid certain kinds of people. Had they been more involved with academic work, maybe their paths would have been totally different, but I wanted them to experience life and not be restricted. It's a bit of a balancing act to guide them even today without telling them what to do. They both hate being restricted, but I still have the instinct of motherly protection. When I compare it to my childhood, I'm very proud that I always kept them safe and with me, no matter what happened around us.

When I reflect on those early years, and look out the window at where we live now, I think to myself, "How we ended up where we are today is really an absolutely bananas journey." I've come a long way since they were babies. I don't need a man in my life, and I don't need a lot of people around me. Given the choice between going to a party and mingling with loads of people or sitting at home with the girls or the dogs, and a bottle of Prosecco watching Netflix, I'd choose the dogs and the girls every time. There was one particular dog that put me on the path to where I am now. Her name was Eyes.

Me and Eyes

Zoe and Holly Mae

Zoe and Holly Mae

Zoe and Holly Mae in Spain with two stray puppies

Me and Zoe at Glastonbury Festival

4

RUSHTON DOG RESCUE

I met Eyes, a Doberman-Collie cross, while working with teenagers as part of an outreach programme. They were ones whose parents were never there when they got back from school, so they'd end up walking around in their school uniforms at 9 o'clock at night, eating chips every night for dinner. I started as a volunteer and eventually they took me on in a paid position in the Weymouth area.

This little dog used to walk round the outreach bus all the time, and I'd give her bits of sausage rolls or whatever snacks we gave the kids. Little did I know this dog was going to live with me for the next 14 years. She was an absolutely amazing dog. Her owner, Timothy Mark Rushton, was homeless and together they lived on the streets. He said, "Her name is Eyes. I call her that because when I'm off me head, she looks out for me." I didn't know then that he was a heroin addict. I didn't really understand an awful lot about that because I was brought up in the Grange Hill "Just Say No" era, so that lifestyle was always something that I kept very well away from. Tim and I became friendly, and I began bringing him clean clothes or whatever else he needed. I naively thought that if I took him back home and gave him a bath and a good night's sleep, everything would be fine.

From there, it all went into another rollercoaster because then I decided I was going to fall head over heels in love with this guy. He was ever so good looking with his goatee and his lovely dark hair and he was a sweet, cheeky chap. I knew he had problems, but I thought I could fix him and that everything was going to be great.

I left the outreach programme when I met him and found work as an auxiliary nurse at the local hospital. Deep down, I knew he was probably never going to see his 35th birthday, but I hung in there even when everyone said I was absolutely bonkers and asked, "What the hell are you doing?" I said, "I don't know. All I know is I've just got to do this." It was such a strong feeling that I had. I just had to see this through, and I didn't know the reason for it. I just knew I had to be involved with this guy. He wasn't horrible to me or anything like that. He was clean for a long time. Then, he relapsed before getting clean for a long time again.

He never brought any drugs into the house. Holly became quite fond of him but Zoe was always a bit leery. She probably thought, "What's Mum doing now?" Part of me knew that it probably wasn't a good thing to bring an addict around my daughters but I just couldn't stop myself and I knew we wouldn't be together forever. My inner self was telling me, "Just follow this path. You've just got to stick with this." I literally just pushed back against all my critics and said, "Stop telling me what to do. I've got to this. I don't know why. I just do." I'm so glad I did because to be fair, that was the first time in my life that I really stood up for myself. It must have looked bonkers from the outside looking in, but in the long run, I definitely did the right thing.

The last time he relapsed, it was December 23rd, the day before Christmas Eve. We had had a bit of a disagreement, he stormed off with Eyes and I never saw him alive again. He went into a public toilet and overdosed. The police found Eyes and brought her to me. It was a funny time because after Tim's death, I almost felt like there was a purpose in our being together. He was the person that set me free from all the stuff that was going on in my head because I became so absorbed with him and all his drama that all of a sudden, my life seemed very simple.

When he died, I felt a warm cloak cover me. I went to the hospital mortuary on Boxing Day to see him and told the police not to contact his parents, whom I had met a few times before. I had promised Tim that if anything ever happened to him, I would never let the police knock on his family's door and tell them he was dead. If there was bad news, it would come from me. After I did him up, I got in my van and I drove to his parents' home in the village of Priddy in Somerset.

I knocked on his parents' door and told them that their

son was he was dead. That was a really difficult day. I'm still friends with his mum and brother today. His dad passed away a few years ago. After that, it was almost like I gained a new perspective on life. I still did some crazy stuff, but it all started to make sense. Things just started to happen that were out of my control, but they were all things that ultimately led me to starting the rescue. Tim and I always talked about starting an animal rescue in Spain to help dogs like Eyes. After his death, bizarrely, animals just started turning up, starting with a little Yorkie with no teeth that a neighbour needed me to look after. Her name was Zoe, which I thought was fate's way of telling me I was on the right path. Then there was another called Alfie and then another after him. Soon after, I heard about a place in Wales that was closing down and they needed to place all these cats. Bearing in mind, we didn't have social media back then, I rang this woman and offered my help. She asked if I had a cattery and I didn't so I moved out of my bedroom and put all the crates in the bedroom and set it up nicely. When the two Welsh women turned up with all the cats, I slept downstairs on the bloody sofa! I didn't realise yet really what I was doing but it was good. Instead of spending all my energy searching for a man or seeking out external experiences, I put all my energy into caring for all these animals. I didn't need to search for anything because I had every single thing I needed including my daughters. It was like some universal force picked me up, blew fresh air on me and then put me back down and I thought, "Oh! Alright, then." Since then, I haven't stopped making vulnerable animals my priority. It was really bizarre as if Tim's death had kicked off this big change and the animals somehow knew to come to me.

I quit my job at the hospital because after seeing him in the mortuary, I never wanted to set foot in the place again and went to work for a mobile phone company. I really enjoyed that for a few years. It was something totally different to what I'd ever done before. I was all suited and booted and walking to work every day. But then the dog thing kind of started to overtake it, and I had to get a second job delivering Chinese takeaways to help pay for the vet bills.

I never set out to rescue dogs. It just evolved really naturally. Rescuing animals isn't something you wake up in the morning and say, "I know what! I'll start a dog rescue today." It wasn't like that. It really just happened. They needed me and I needed them.

Animals had been a comfort to me when I was a little girl when my mother would leave me alone with Tara the Afghan hound for hours on end. Tara was my first real friend and protector. Later, when my foster parents threw me out, I shut myself off emotionally from animals for a long time. It wasn't just the pain of losing my pony and the other farm animals but because the whole situation was almost too painful to think about. I tried to block it all out and ignore that pain for many years.

Tim's death gave me what I needed. I tried to be there for him, but he couldn't be the person I wanted him to be because addiction had taken over in such a powerful way that it was just horrible. I wouldn't wish that on anyone. It's the most awful thing to watch someone killing themselves through any kind of addiction. Whether it's through drugs, anorexia, or self-harm, it's very, very sad to watch someone destroy themselves that way. When he died, I didn't die with him. I came alive. His death gave me what I had been searching for my whole life. It gave me a purpose that had nothing to do with men. This was the path I was meant to take with the animals and I would never have discovered that had I not met him.

Had I not been a youth worker and subsequently not met Tim and Eyes on the street, then I wouldn't be where I am today. Had I not taken him home, given him a bath, fallen in love with him, lost him and taken in Eyes, then none of what happened after would have and countless other lives would not have been saved.

In those early days, if I took a little dog then I saw that it was my responsibility at that point to go and pay for the vet bills, so I'd do whatever I had to in order to pay those bills. I worked a lot because we didn't have social media where I could fundraise and I wasn't very good at asking for help. I have never been that good at that. I've always thought, "Well, if I took this on then it's my responsibility."

A few years later, I literally did wake up one morning

feeling overwhelmed with all these animals thinking, "What the heck am I going to do? Maybe I should make this into a bloody charity!" I knew that if I was going to go down that road, I had to do it the right way. I knew I had to set everything properly. In 2007, I officially established The Rushton Dog Rescue charity – named after Timothy, the man who changed my life.

In the early days of the charity, I went back and forth to Ireland a lot and rescued many farm dogs who had lived very difficult lives. We have had many bumps along the way since our inception. It took me a long time to put our PayPal details up on our website because I still felt I wasn't worthy of anyone's help. It took me a really long time to get my head around the idea of asking for help. I think a lot of that is to do with believing in yourself and again, not wanting to ask for something for fear of rejection. I wanted to avoid that feeling of rejection. All these years later, Zoe still says I have trouble asking for help for even the smallest things.

Another challenge I had to overcome was the issue of setting up foster homes for the animals I was rescuing. I have never had that much patience with people. That was my downfall. I was never really good with the whole foster thing because I used to find myself getting quite irritated with people who would bring a dog back to me because his or her dog was having an issue in a home. Some people just expected the dog to be perfectly well-behaved, but that's not how it works any more than it worked that way in *my* foster home. Back then, I didn't understand why people couldn't deal with it. From my point of view, it was perfectly natural for a dog who came from an abusive or unstable environment to have behavioural problems. I'm not running down the people who helped me back then but it didn't take me long to separate the wheat from the chaff, let's put it that way. Sadly, I had no choice but to put them in all these foster homes because we didn't have anywhere else to keep them at that time. The girls and I struggled for a long time to find a place to live in the UK as we took more dogs in.

In 2010, we opened a charity shop on Portland Road in Wyke Regis just outside Weymouth which we still have today. We accept donations and all the proceeds go towards the care and feeding of our dogs. It used to be a pet shop actually, and I used to go up and see the owner all the time and I always said to him. "If you ever give up the shop, let me know because it will make a great charity shop." Someone beat me to it, but they didn't last five minutes. Then, we managed to get it, and we've rented it ever since. It's a lovely shop. I've had the same people working there for the past 11 years including Sam, our manager.

For the most part, people give us clothes and books and all the normal charity shop bric-a-brac, but there was one item that stands out as being quite memorable. One day, Sam got a call from the family of an elderly lady who had passed away. She went around to pick up the items at the deceased woman's home and spotted a vintage Hornby train set in the corner. Immediately, she thought, "Oh! That'll bring in a few quid for the charity!" The family stopped her and said, "No, not that! *This* is yours," then handed her a box filled with old Tupperware on top of which rested an old prosthetic leg, dangling like a crime scene leftover. She looked at the family and said, "I don't think there's going to be very many one-legged people shopping for a new limb in a charity shop. There's not much call for it, really." Disappointed, they said, "Well, we thought you might be able to use it." Sam called me up and said, "You're not going to believe this one…"

Even with the shop bringing in money, we still had trouble housing the ever-growing number of dogs. For a while, we moved the charity to Spain and ran it from there. We did a lot of good work there, rescuing about 900 dogs in total. We liberated many hunting dogs who had been permanently chained outside farmhouses, and fed with only the occasional bit of bread up in the mountain villages. I would send the dogs back to different rescues in the UK. I learned a lot about myself, too. In Spain, I could feel my commitment to helping animals growing even stronger. I loved being the rescuer with the hands-on, boots-on-the-ground work that this entailed, but even more, I loved everything else that followed including working with the animals individually and finding them a suitable home. Anyone can rescue a dog, but it's what you do with it after that counts.

We stayed there for about three years and then I went to France for about six months where I rented a small cottage on my own with the dogs in the middle of nowhere. About three months in, Eyes passed away. It was horrible. She had an internal tumour that erupted and burst in the middle of the night. I rushed around trying to find someone who was British and who spoke French to help me, but poor old Eyes didn't make it. A few weeks later, our cat Mitzi, who we'd had since the girls were little, died at the age of 18.

The loss of these two important family members sunk me into a very deep depression. There I was in the French countryside, on my own with all these dogs to look after while Holly and Zoe were back in the UK.

When the UK referendum to leave the EU took place, it created a lot of uncertainty. With Brexit looming, I decided to move back home to a nice, but entirely unsuitable rented farmhouse in Somerset. It was probably the most unfriendly hamlet we ever lived in. No one wanted us there.

On our rented property, a lot of dogs often struggled to adapt regardless of where they came from. The ones who didn't became permanent residents. Many rescues are semi-feral and extremely fearful of humans. In short, all of them had different issues that needed addressing. I soon realised there was no "one size fits all" remedy.

Ironically, I have always found that it's the dogs who come from "normal" homes that often have the worst behaviours – all of which they picked up from their humans. A lot of them were left alone home all day long while their caregivers were at work, so they have anxiety and trust issues/ Sounds familiar, doesn't it?

By this time, I understood that the best course of action was to look after as many dogs as I could and get to know each one individually before deciding on a good forever home for them. I didn't want a third party to get to know those dogs and then have the dog moved again into a "permanent" home. To this day, I want to be in a position where I can look at a dog…I mean really look at them, love them, nurture them, and find out what kind of home and human family they are best suited for. The only way to do this would be to have an even bigger property with lots of outside space for exercise and inside space for kennels. After all the stress and loss of the previous few years, all I wanted was to be settled and have a home.

Hercules and Me

Me and Alfie

Zoë in China with Crystal

Me at a shelter in Chengdu

Me and some of the beloved rescue dogs

A YOUNG man was found dead in a toilet cubicle in Weymouth town centre, an inquest was told.

Timothy Rushton, 28, died in the toilets by the Town Bridge on the day before Christmas Eve.

West Dorset Coroner Michael Johnston recorded a verdict of accidental death after describing the death as incredibly sad.

The inquest in Dorchester was told that a man found Mr Rushton in the cubicle when he heard a dog barking behind the door.

Graham Robinson said: "I climbed on to the urinal to see who was in there and I saw a man I know as Mark. There was a needle on the floor."

Mr Robinson said that he tried to climb into the cubicle but was not able to.

By ECHO REPORTER

echodorch@dorsetecho.co.uk

The inquest was told that Mr Robinson then called the police from a nearby pay phone.

He said he knew Tim Rushton, who was homeless and also known as Mark, through the 'Weymouth drug scene'.

Saddest

He added: "I feel sick, with my own drug taking, to see what it can do to you."

The coroner told the Dorchester inquest that heroin, alcohol and diazepam had been found in Mr Rushton's blood.

Looking at pictures taken at the Town Bridge toilets, Mr Johnson said: "These are some of the saddest photographs I've seen for a long time.

"That a young man should end his life in a cubicle of a public toilet seems to me incredibly, incredibly sad."

He added: "Unfortunately he may not have known the effect of combining alcohol, heroin and diazepam.

"They are a potentially fatal combination because all act as central nervous system depressants."

Mr Johnson recorded a verdict of accidental death and praised Mr Rushton's former girlfriend, auxiliary nurse Cindi McNeil, for helping him with his addiction.

He said: "Thank you for what you tried to do for him and with him to try to get him to stop using."

Campaigners called for a homeless shelter soon after Mr Rushton's death but Miss McNeil questioned whether it would have been of help to Mr Rushton.

Newspaper clipping of Tim's passing

Our beautiful Eyes

5

FREEDOM FARM

When we found Freedom Farm, it was equipped with everything we needed. We rallied around all our core supporters and the Rushton Dog Rescue Charity trustees. Everybody did their bit, and we managed to pull enough money together to move in. This book would not be complete if I didn't mention the incredible loyalty of our supporters. People can talk and talk about giving and charity but the proof of the pudding is in the eating. We could not have moved here without every single one of our supporters. They pulled out all the stops, and we got the deposit together. The trustees sorted the mortgage out, and that was it. Freedom Farm was ours on 31st March 2020 – four days after the UK went into lockdown because of the COVID-19 pandemic.

Zoe and I had to move here on our own with all the animals in one van. Once we had everything moved, I thought to myself, "Right. This is going to be a real home for us." For the first time in my life, I could use the word "home" and really mean it. After years of being bounced around from place to place as a child and then searching and wandering as an adult, I had finally found the balance of freedom and security that I had longed for.

Although lockdown created challenges in terms of fundraising, in a weird way it was kind of the best thing that could have happened for us because it gave me time to settle in and create a routine for the dogs before we had people popping in constantly for adoptions. I'm an ambivert – quite an outgoing person, but also very introverted. I love my own company. I'm not a person who wants people stopping by when I've got no time for them. I'm here for the animals and they are my priority. Always.

We've got so much space here that every day the dogs all come out and they can all walk in the fields for hours on end. Some dogs here now used to be street dogs, so it's really nice for them because they come here and feel the grass beneath their paws and the fresh air on their faces. It's like a village for dogs with safety protocols in place.

Inside, they've all got their nice comfy little beds, their chew toys, blankets, and whatever else they need. Some rescuers obsess over numbers and concentrate on finding homes for dogs as quickly as possible. We all want these dogs to find lovely homes, of course. But some dogs can't actually cope with it. If a dog gets adopted and bounces back to me once or twice for behavioural issues, that's it. I never put them out there again. I don't believe in constantly putting them out into a life of rotating chaos. Our adoption process at Rushton concentrates on what's right for each dog.

I take an individual-centred approach towards each dog. I am not concerned with the number of dogs placed into homes, rather whether it is the *right* home for that dog. We match them with a family based on their individual temperaments and experiences and we adopt out only when the match is suitable to a level that the dog will not likely be returned to us. They've been through enough already and don't need further chaos.

We don't rush into anything. It is not possible for someone to just drive up, pick a dog and take it home on the same day as it is at some shelters. The application process to adopt a dog from Rushton is a rigorous one. After an initial application is filled out, we review it and then conduct both phone and in-person interviews. Then the applicant meets the dog here on the property under supervision and either Zoe or I show them around and explain everything.

The dogs either live with them or they live with us. There's no in between. It's contracted so that the dog won't be left with neighbours or relatives or anything like that. When we take an animal in, we become that dog's umbrella. We look that animal in the eyes and say, "I will protect you for the rest of your days, no matter when you find a home, or if you stay here. Whatever happens, we will look after you. You are safe here and you are loved."

If the initial meeting with an applicant goes well, Zoe

or I – or sometimes both of us – will visit the person's home to ensure they have enough indoor and outdoor space depending on the needs of the dog and that all the information they've given us is true to the best of their knowledge. Sadly, there are some nefarious people out there who will adopt a dog only to try to sell it on, making all our checks necessary.

The next stage in the process involves Zoe and me driving the dog to the applicant's home the following week to spend a few hours with the applicant to see how the dog and the person interact in the environment together. Impatience with the adoption process is usually a tell-tale sign that this person is not a good fit for one of our dogs. I tell everyone that these animals are precious. If they were children, no one would ever think twice about spending this much time getting the right match. I am giving attention to the details that should have been given in my situation when I was a child.

If a person-centred approach like this one had been taken with my case (or countless others) within the British care system, I likely wouldn't have acted out the way I did. Since the '70s, a more person-centred approach within the care system in the UK has led to improvements for the younger generations. Today, the system prioritises the children with the planning and decisions that affect their lives, health and mental well-being much more than they did when I was growing up.

To me, applying these methods to working with abandoned, neglected or abused animals is just common sense. I wake up every day and see the results in the eyes of the dogs I work with. It's so wonderful to speak to someone who's kind and understands what we're trying to accomplish here at Freedom Farm.

When a dog at Freedom Farm finds a forever home, it's the best feeling in the world. I love getting progress reports on our dogs and their new families. Every family who adopts from us becomes a member of the Rushton family. Rarely do we have dogs returned to us, but we have had a few sad cases where the person became ill or passed away. Then the family will say, "We know the dog was always meant to come back to you," and at that point I say to the dog, "Let me keep you safe now," because that's what it's about.

I'm fiercely protective of where my dogs go. Some of the larger breeds need lots of outdoor space to run, some have medical problems, some dogs don't like people, while others don't like other animals or children. They all have distinct personalities. Some form incredibly strong bonds that cannot be broken and so they can only be adopted as a pair.

Freedom Farm offers sanctuary where the dogs feel safe and loved. We spend so much time with them that we get to know very quickly when they are ready to be adopted Some will stay here forever. The result in working this way is that when I find a good home, it's really forever. I've had a few families call us for second or third dogs years later after a first dog we'd matched them with passed away after living long, happy lives. Recently, we spoke to a gentleman on the phone who was the father-in-law of a couple that adopted one dog we rescued from China earlier this year. That's a project worthy of its own chapter!

Over the years, we've rescued and homed over 4,000 dogs. Eyes acted as our mascot, dutifully watching over us until she passed away a few years ago at the ripe old age of 14. Tim's probably up in the sky right now, looking down, thinking, "Well done!" I know he'd be proud of the way we run things here.

Happy days at Freedom Farm before the rain came!

Zoe, Me, Kemp, Panda and Edith

From left to right: Jasmine, Ariel, Talula, Pandora and Marina in the back

Freedom Farm

6

THE DARKNESS TO LIGHT PROJECT

A common joke I heard growing up was that if someone's dog or cat disappeared, we could find them at the local Chinese restaurant on the menu. Unfortunately, the reality is far from humorous. Millions of animals are born and live horrible lives before dying and being served in restaurants to paying customers. They keep beautiful dogs in a prison where their fate is the worst imaginable, stacked on top of each other in concrete cells. Often, there are up to 20 dogs in each cell like something out of a horror film, all fearing for what is to come next. Can you imagine how petrified they must be? Then, they load the dogs into cramped travel cages and load hundreds of them onto a truck. The lucky ones are rescued off the backs of these transport lorries by caring members of the Chinese public. The others are taken to the slaughterhouse to be murdered.

Rescuing them is only the first step. Most people don't

think about where the dogs go after being taken off the lorries. Most end up in crowded shelters in the countryside with little hope of finding a forever home in China. This is the end of the road for most dogs. There will be no new family to cuddle and play with. Most will live out their remaining years in overcrowded conditions, never knowing the feeling of grass beneath their paws. Over time, their health will gradually deteriorate from lack of sufficient food, not to mention the risk of distemper and other communicable diseases, fleas, ticks and the constant danger of attack from other dogs.

I've always wanted to get involved with rescuing dogs from the Chinese meat trade. In 2016, I was finally in a position to do it. We helped the Chinese meat trade dogs that year when we started to hear the horrendous truth of what happens over there. The dog meat trade in China is massive, and it's happening 365 days of the year. You may have heard of the Yulin Festival where dogs are slaughtered in horrific ways and their bodies are sold at a market to consumers. Most people believe that the Yulin Festival is the only time of the year when dogs are slaughtered but unfortunately, it happens every day.

Hopefully, with the passage of time, China will change for the better and begin to treat dogs and other animals with greater respect. For now, we will keep fighting. But we can't do it alone. Every donation we receive helps. We won't stop until we feel we have done enough and we can assure you that isn't going to be for a very long time.

When the dogs are rescued, they are taken to a vet to see what damage has been caused by their ordeal. We pay to put them into boarding where they can start to build strength, gain weight and generally becoming healthier so that they can travel to us in the UK to begin their new lives and go up for adoption. It takes many hours and a lot of money to bring these dogs here, but it's worth every minute and pound when they arrive from the airport.

Zoe and I have each travelled separated to China. It's always heart breaking to walk into the huge, barren shelters where all the dogs just run around in one big open space. There are literally hundreds of them who need proper homes, each one having endured incredible pain and yearning for freedom with expectant gazes, wagging tails and barks. Despite their physical differences, they all had one thing in common: they had all come to live in shelters having been rescued from butchers, meat markets and smoke-filled, dirty city streets. They had all lived lives devoid of human affection. Many experienced beatings, strangulation and torture. For them, this shelter was the first place they'd ever known safety from the violence of humankind. I could see in their eyes that each one was grateful to be alive, but there is more to life than simply existing. These souls deserved more than that. I've held and stroked so many dogs in China that I've lost count. Even though they all had unique physical and psychological problems, they all needed love.

I've met dogs from all over the world, but the dogs from China are generally the most grateful for what they're given once they arrive here at Freedom Farm. Many of them are older dogs, with some being 14 or 15 but they are incredibly strong dogs who have endured a lot in their lives. They are both the hardest dogs to look after and the easiest in different ways. It takes a lot of time and money to bring them to Rushton and once they are here, many of them are very fearful of humans because of their experiences in the meat trade. They all have very different needs at different levels but in general, they integrate quite easily with other dogs because they've been kept in groups their entire lives, albeit in horridly cramped spaces. When they come here, we give them time to decompress, each in their own time.

The reformation of the Chinese system comes down to improving education. Even as the global movement towards respect for our natural world and animal life grows, there is a need to educate people in China on the plight of their country's meat trade. Hopefully, as each generation becomes more educated on the subject of animal cruelty and neglect, attitudes will change. I know that the work we are doing will not end in my lifetime. All we can do is try to make a difference one dog at a time, ensuring their stories take a positive turn. Freedom Farm is a sanctuary for them and for all dogs that need help. A place for them to run, play, rest, and be safe from the cruelties of their past lives.

7

DOG TALES

First and foremost, Freedom Farm is about its residents. Although my personal story has featured prominently in this book, it's their stories that serve as inspiration for us to do what we do every day. All our residents are special and unique individuals. This chapter is all about them.

Toby

I got Toby when I was living in Spain. In English, he's a Jack Russell terrier but in Spain, they're known as "bodeguero." He still lives with me today. A fair had just come through town and I spotted him with a chain around his neck. When the fair upped sticks and left town, they left Toby behind to wander the streets, making a nuisance of himself. He had a bit of a limp and was nothing but skin and bone. Nobody could get near him. His howling drove everyone nuts, so people started throwing water over him from their apartments. I put a trap in one of the underground car parks to try to see if I could catch him. It went on for weeks anyway, and then eventually I got a phone call from a German couple who said they'd seen him in our Camino. He'd walked right out of town. We managed to herd him into their villa compound behind the electric gates, but it still took ages to catch him. I was running around yelling, "Get me a cover! Just get me something!" I finally threw a duvet over him, grabbed him and threw him in the back of my Jeep. To this day, I can barely touch a hair on this dog's head. He has an airgun pellet embedded in his ear and, as a result, is the most antisocial dog I've come across in all my days. He does not like people and is an absolute hellraiser this dog. He's neurotic and has funny phobias. He won't walk on a floor if it's really shiny, so I've put mats down in a few places. He has to live on the other side of my house with one of my other dogs, Jeffrey, because he's really moody. He isn't a dog that was ever going to go into someone's home. It's impossible to put a collar or lead on him, so that is never going to happen, but I've kept him safe. He's got his own garden and sofa. He's very complex psychologically, but his needs are very simple and only Zoe or I can deal with him.

LOVEY

Lovey was a victim of street abuse in China in the province of Wuhan. Targeted and tortured as a young pup, she has lost part of her beautiful face as a result. Our greatest dream for Lovey would be if we could get her in to see Professor Noel Fitzpatrick, the world-class Irish orthopaedic-neuro veterinary surgeon, for a consultation to see if there is anything he could do to make her more comfortable. She lives a noble life. She can eat, drink and definitely chew – that's for sure! However, her nasal breathing passage is so narrow that she breathes through her mouth most of the time. Working with Professor Fitzpatrick would have the added benefit of shining a spotlight on the dogs suffering in China and help to raise awareness of all the work that needs to be done there.

George

As of summer 2021, George has been with us for close to a year now. A little black mixed-breed dog, it's taken him a while to calm down from his ordeal in China but we can tell he's almost ready to be adopted. He's come so far emotionally since he first arrived here. He was very nervous and confrontational at the beginning, but we've let him decompress and have taken the time to get to know him. George, like many of our rescues from China, needed time to get to know himself. These animals don't know who they are. They don't know whether they like to share. They don't know what toys they want to play with. They don't know whether they're tired in the morning or the afternoon or if they want to play in the field or what they will do once they are in the field because they've never been in a field before. If you keep a dog in a metal crate for their entire life, how can they possibly know themselves? George has made great strides since joining us and we look forward to the day when he's ready to live the loving life he deserves.

BG & Jupiter

One of the most beautiful things that happens here at Rushton is the friendships and bonds the dogs develop. BG and Jupiter are an inseparable pair, having both been saved from China. BG is a solo survivor, where she was found in a bag at the back of a meat truck. Jupiter was in Shanghai near a construction site at great danger of being captured by the meat traders, but thankfully he was rescued in time.

Both of these babies live at Freedom Farm with Zoe and me. Actually, they live inside my house with me and my pack! From the first moment these two met, they've been in love, but Jupiter definitely made all the first moves! Whether they are from the same country when they come here or not, they all merge into one big, great, happy family. Our family.

Baggy

Baggy is my little disabled mixed girl from China. Both of her back legs were damaged after being hit by a truck, although she can still walk a bit. She lives with me as part of the pack of dogs who will never leave Freedom Farm. Even though she's only been with us a short while, I absolutely love her. She has the sweetest personality and loves to cuddle on my lap and sleep on my bed. She's got mammary cancer and had surgery to remove the whole lot from top to bottom. She recovered very well even at her age, which is probably 12 or 13 years old. She was so small when she first came to us, she looked absolutely dreadful but now she's built-up muscle and is nice and healthy looking. She's just amazing.

Iris

Iris is a little brown toy poodle who came to us from China and found her forever home in the home of Shirlie and Martin Kemp. Imagine being stuck in a crate one day and then, after spending time with us, going on to live an extremely posh life! It was an excellent match.

Ting Tong

Ting Tong was a little Pomeranian we rescued from a shelter in Shanghai. He was an old boy. The first time I met him, I picked him up and said, "Hello, darling! I've looked so forward to meeting you," and kissed him on the nose. He replied by biting *my* nose with his little toothless mouth. Zoe was laughing her head off. It was love at first sight after that and we became the best of friends. When he first arrived at Freedom Farm, he had no hair but as it grew back in, he had all these little ginger bits of fluff on him. He was a bit of a celebrity and came everywhere with me. He had multiple hernia operations and passed away just a few months after joining us. Everybody loved Ting Tong – the little legend!

Beau

We rescued Beau, an older shepherd with a history of biting, last year from being put to sleep locally. He has settled into his new life at Freedom Farm and now resides in the VIP suite with the ladies, which makes him a very happy chap! His favourite ball is his red Kong ball. Wherever the ball goes, so does Beau!

Parker

Parker is a perfect example of a mixed dog we took in that would have never had a chance elsewhere. He's an old boy we brought in from China who had been living with a broken/ fused bone in his leg for years. We knew from the outset that he wouldn't be put up for adoption. I brought him out to give him two square meals a day, a sofa, his own space, and so that he would no longer have to live in fear. I remember being in the shelter and saying to the lady in China (with the help of my translator), "I want him." She looked at me like I was crazy and said, "But there's all these younger, purebred dogs." I said, "No, I want to take *him*." She protested, "We can't catch him." I persisted, "We'll have to dart him, then." He'd been there seven years, surrounded by thousands of others, and was completely written off. Half of one of his ears was chewed off, and he was just completely nondescript amongst all the others. 90% of people wouldn't notice him. The lady who ran the shelter couldn't believe I wanted him. He's now living in one of the big huts up at the top of the farm with his own bit of grass and an old sofa to lounge on. He doesn't mix with the other dogs, but he's perfectly content to relax and watch the goings on. Dogs like Parker need more help than the younger, fancier breeds in shelters. It's really not that different from the children like me who were ignored in the care system in the 1970s. These parallels are not lost on me.

Me and Kemp

Meat truck that BG was in, in China

Kemp's new family

Me, Shirlie and Iris, and Zoe

8

PARALLELS

All that I do every single day comes from being a little girl who was shifted around from place to place until I finally ended up in a house that was not a home. To the British care system, I was little more than a statistic. A number on paper who was constantly told, "Don't do this, don't do that." Living that way can fuck your whole life up later on. No one was able to read my acting out as a symptom of my abuse in my foster home. It was a mystery to everyone around me, including myself, for a great deal of my young adult life. It is no longer a mystery to me.

During my childhood, I acted out because of all the chaos and abuse in my life and was deemed a "bad" kid. I carried that "bad kid" mentality throughout my adolescence and into early adulthood, recreating the chaos by choosing peers and romantic partners who were not good for me.

Over time, I came to realise that I wasn't "bad", I was just a kid with a tremendous amount of chaos and instability in my life and acting out is a natural consequence of that. I've seen this dynamic play out over and over with neglected and abused dogs. I don't see an aggressive dog as "bad." I see them as having gone through horrible experiences to where they no longer trust, and in some cases, deeply fear the companionship of human beings. I understand them completely. Every day I wake up determined to be the person that I needed as a child and who the dogs at Freedom Farm need today.

We have learned to read the behaviour of our animals at Rushton and do something for them that those around me never did for me. I find out what they need, and hopefully make informed decisions for their well-being. Zoe and I are grateful every day that we have this place, which allows us the freedom and time to get to know each dog so that they don't become a statistic like I did.

Homing a child or a dog for the sake of homing them without getting to know their personality or finding out who the adopting family is on a deeper level is not good. Taking the time and putting in the effort is something that we can really pride ourselves on here at Freedom Farm because we now finally have the space to keep those dogs for longer rather than just get them in and out as a statistic.

If just one person had tried a little harder to make a difference in my life when I was in the care system, it would have made all the difference in the world. Inaction beyond the level of box-ticking in the face of an overwhelmed, poorly run, underfunded system has led to negative outcomes for thousands of children like me in the areas of physical health, emotional and mental health, as well as educational, economic and professional achievement. Many people who grow up to be abused and neglected become abusers themselves, not only of their own children but ironically also of animals. The situations are not only parallel but connected. Neglect and abuse have long-reaching consequences as much as do kindness and empathy. If a child is shown kindness and empathy, they are more likely to grow up to be the type of person who is kind to animals.

What happens in your childhood often comes back to haunt you later in life, but how you deal with that is up to you. Don't be a bloody victim. I'm a survivor, not a victim. Through my work with animals, I changed negatives into positives, and put all the knowledge I've gained through the challenging lessons I've learned into helping those who, although they may be four-footed, share a lot in common with me.

I've talked a lot about how I was bounced around and homed with the wrong family–these are two of the things I share in common with the animals at Rushton. Another way is in terms of "breeding". When I was a little girl, no one wanted me because I was mixed-race. My own maternal relatives rejected me partly for being half Egyptian. This parallels the obsession some people have with purebred animals.

When a person calls up and enquires about a specific dog on our website, one of the first questions I always ask is "What experience have you got with dogs?" If their answer starts with, "I used to breed X and Y," then I absolutely will not consider them as a suitable person for one of our dogs. I have a strict anti-breeding policy and all of our dogs are spayed or neutered before being homed.

None of the dogs at Freedom Farm had a choice in being born into their genetic or environmental circumstances any more than I did. When I was a child in it up to my neck, I couldn't see the bigger picture. I couldn't see the systemic indifference partially to blame for my circumstances. Now I realise there are changes that both the animal rescue system and the UK care system could implement to effect positive change.

The best thing that could happen to animals is if the government were to regulate the rescue system. Right now, I think it's too easy for people to get a dog that isn't spayed or neutered. Our government needs to step up their policies on breeding. They say it's got better since Lucy's Law came into effect in 2020, which banned the sale of dogs from third parties and limited the sale of puppies and kittens from breeders, but all it's done is driven the dubious sellers underground and made "official" breeding more profitable. During lockdown, there was a record number of dog thefts in London and the thieves put most of them up for sale on the black market. As long as people see animals as a commodity, it will continue to be a worldwide problem that will not slow down soon. Here at Freedom Farm, our dogs are treated as the individual precious souls they are. We take everyone – even the dog with a broken leg, the one that's incontinent, and the one that you're never going to touch. They are all living beings who desire the same things we all do: safety, happiness, a full belly and a roof over our heads.

What is most interesting are the similar coping mechanisms that both abandoned children and animals exhibit. I have spoken a great deal about my mistrust of people. It's the same with dogs. It's completely logical. Why would you trust people if all they've ever shown you is cruelty and/or indifference? It takes a long time for me to open up to people and trust them, so I completely understand it when I meet a new dog who regards me with suspicion.

The care system in the UK has improved since my time, with increased awareness of abuse, and stricter vetting processes to keep situations like mine from being common. In today's system, a little girl would never be placed in a home where her bedroom didn't have its own door and they would likely tackle many of the anger problems I experienced with counselling. I think, with greater funding, an individual-based approach would be successful in reducing the number of children bounced from home to home because of behavioural problems. We really need to think about what's best for a child rather than just ticking a box. Getting the match right with a foster family would save everyone a lot of time and money and lead to happier children overall.

There is no point in dwelling on what could have been. The past is the past. I live my life today, as the person I needed in my life when I was small. I'm not perfect, but judging from the results, I'm sure I'm on the right path.

9

EVERY SOUL MATTERS

The first thing I do in the morning after waking up to furry licks and cuddles between 5am and 6am is let my 14 permanent-resident dogs out. All of these dogs have lived with me in my house for years and can't be adopted out for various reasons. They're what we call "The First Team." I grab a cup of coffee and quickly check my emails while The First Team is outside doing their thing. Then, I'm straight out into the yard with Zoe to sort the yard dogs out.

We have many things that we have to do here daily, from vet visits to endless rounds of cleaning and washing. We feed them (some require a special diet), give them any medication they need, clean up after them and start taking them out of their kennels into groups for their daily exercise. They roam around, running and playing for hours in the morning. We normally stop around half past 9 or 10am, at which point, we grab a piece of toast and another cup of coffee. Early afternoon from around noon until 3pm is what I call "the lull time" before the afternoon exercise and play period, although it is really anything but relaxing. This is when we check the emails for adoption applications and when we normally meet with families in person looking to adopt and travel out to their homes to make sure the environment is suitable.

We've also got a few other animals on the farm further down on the property in their own area separate from the dogs who need looking after. Currently, we've got one horse, a big mare named Molly and four little Shetlands, one of whom I named Folly, just like the one I had growing up. We rescued another Shetland in during the 2020-2021 national pandemic lockdown who looked a bit porky when she arrived and now she's had a baby. The horses are called Dolly, Polly, Folly, Tommy and the mare Molly. Of course, we can't forget Holly! We've also got two ducks called Marylin and Audrey. It's a lot of work, but we love it.

Every soul matters. Sometimes, when an animal first arrives, I can see so much pain and fear in their face that it's overwhelming. I just want to pick them up, hug them and wipe away their past. I know that's not possible, but I can confidently say we've saved thousands of lives since our inception and we do our best, every day to create a homely atmosphere for the dogs, regardless of how much time they might spend with us. Even the dogs who are terminally ill appreciate all the love and attention they get in their twilight months. I have never understood people who only want to adopt puppies. I understand that puppies are great, but elderly dogs and those with chronic illnesses love no less than a puppy. For many, a dog is little more than a fashion accessory or something to cuddle.

It never ceases to amaze me when people call asking if they can come and "look at the dogs." Freedom Farm is not a zoo. These dogs live here. It's their home, and it's my home. Who wants to be stared at while they're going about their day? With everyone's best interests at heart, our gates are shut unless you have an appointment. We want to be sensitive to the needs of the dogs who are afraid of strangers and we don't want our dogs paraded around like commodities. A rescue should take dogs because the dog needs help, but far too often, it's people who need a dog to help them feel something or look a certain way.

It takes a very special kind of person to do the work we do every day. It's messy, physically demanding and it requires a great deal of patience. When a dog becomes ill or passes on, it's emotional. Some people think they can just rock up and volunteer casually and that it will be all cuddles and chew toys. I assure you, there's plenty of shit to shovel! There's grass to be cut and weeds to be pulled. That's the kind of thing we need done for us. There are always people who want to do things for their own gratification, but those aren't the people who are suited to working with animals, in my opinion. There are days when Zoe and I give every ounce of ourselves to the dogs from sunrise to sunset and after that... we answer emails! It is literally a 24-7, seven-days-a-week job. There are no holidays and no dinners out. This is our life. We give it everything. To run a rescue properly, you will have no social life. If you're the kind of person who likes to ease into the day slowly with a shower, breakfast and meditation, this definitely isn't the job for you!

There are barely enough hours in the day for what goes on here and each day is unpredictable from hour to hour. One minute, you'll be doing one thing and then the next minute, someone isn't feeling well and needs a vet visit or there's a new dog that needs our help.

The COIVD-19 lockdown was particularly hard but we had two amazing volunteers who came and helped us while their own business was shut. Now, it's just me and Zoe again, with full days from sunrise to bedtime. We've made a commitment to these dogs and they are our responsibility. I'm so committed that sometimes it's as if there's nothing else out there but this. I haven't had a lie-in in I can't remember when!

Where the Chinese dogs are concerned, lately, I've noticed a lot of people around the world wanting to get involved for the hero status who have no idea how difficult and expensive it is to rescue from China. Many have good intentions but have no idea how difficult it is emotionally and financially. Sadly, there are even people who start the process, put the dogs into boarding and then, when they find out how much it costs, they abandon the project, leaving the dogs no better off than when they started.

I think a lot of people get caught up in seeing the pictures of cute animals online and don't think much deeper than that first emotional reaction. They're naively optimistic about how much help they can give.

It's either in you or it's not in you to do this kind of work. I think some people probably want to get involved because they believe it to be something it isn't, and then when they see the reality of the day-to-day processes of running an animal sanctuary, they realise it's not for them. While you're here, you've got to be fully committed and put everything else on the back burner. I barely have time to answer my mobile some days. There are many people in the world doing wonderful work with animal charities, but it must be understood going in that it's a massive commitment.

For example, if you take a dog in that's two years old, re-home it, and then you decide five years later, "Well, I will not do rescuing anymore. I'm not doing it," what happens when that dog needs you further down the line? What if the owner passes away? There's no backup for them. You can't play at this casually. There are real lives at stake. You can't just say, "Oh, I'll have a go at that for a while" because that's when animals suffer and it doesn't them more harm than good. If you're thinking about how something will make you feel good and virtuous for a short while, then that's not a reason to do it.

That's not to say we haven't worked with some wonderful volunteers. We have worked with some amazing people. We've had some people who have given hours of their time and support. Loyalty is a very big thing for me, having experienced none from my own biological or foster families. Dogs are the most loyal animals on the planet. I completely understand it when a dog has nothing but mistrust for humans. Trust and loyalty are in short supply these days and are not traits that can be cultivated in a short time, especially for someone like me or our residents at Freedom Farm. It takes more than just a couple of weeks for some of these dogs to realise they're going to have full bellies and receive love and attention. We have a wonderful group of people who support Rushton Dog Rescue, including Shirlie Kemp (Martin of Spandau Ballet's wife) who is a patron. It's a strange coincidence because music played such an important role in my life all the way back to the days of keeping a transistor radio under my pillow. They got their dog Iris from us and we named another recent rescue – a Rough Collie after them. Kemp suffered a great ordeal at the hands of meat traders, but we found a great home for him. He was the sweetest lad imaginable, and he absolutely loved his time at Freedom Farm, running with all his mates, playing like crazy and discovering his true Kemp self. Being utterly gorgeous certainly helped, as we had lots of interest in Kemp and very quickly we found the perfect match! Kemp now has a wonderful new family who adores the him. Kemp has already bonded with his "brother" in his new, nice, calm home and enjoys being the centre of attention and finally receiving the love he always needed. We honestly couldn't be happier with our choice of home for him. We're always here for him if Kemp ever needs us, but we're happy to see him living a good life with his new family. It's stories like these that make working so hard worth it.

CONCLUSION

My goal in writing this book was to show how you can change your life around regardless of the circumstances you're born into. You don't have to stay in "that thing" whatever it is. There were people I was in care with that killed themselves and yeah, there were times I wanted to as well. I tried but obviously didn't try hard enough, so it was more of a cry for help. There are people on the street selling The Big Issue, and they've all had these terrible things happen to them. I wanted to show that it's important to count your blessings. I'm very blessed that there was a survival lion inhabiting a part of my DNA. Wherever it came from, it eventually came out and said, "No, I'm not going to be a victim of my past, and I will not sacrifice my future to my past. I'm going to do things on my terms and I don't have to remain a statistical victim."

A person's past shapes who they become only up to a point while always remaining a constant influence in the background. I became the person I needed in my life when I was a child. Whatever you focus on with determination and dedication, that's what your life will become and a lot of the negative experiences that happened in the past will turn into positives. Some of the most successful people in the world have come from a horrific background, and endured the most horrendous abuse. They've gone on to do the most marvellous things with their lives. Like them, I had that inner lion who said, "You are not going to defeat me!"

Life isn't about denying the bad experiences. It's about being able to move forward. It's not until you can actually accept that it's happened and accept the impact it has had on you in all the different paths you have taken and all the people who have come in and out of your life that you really understand the rule of attraction. If you let the past control you, you will continue to attract negative people into your life. Coming to terms with the past will help you to move forward and create a positive future. All of my experiences have made me who I am today.

Obviously, there was plenty of blame to go around, whether it was my mother, her family, my foster parents, my foster brother, or the care system as a whole. For years, they had control of my life and now *I* am in control. They don't get to control it anymore, even if it's just as ghosts from the past. This is why I do what I do at Rushton and live the life I do now. I will no longer be seen and not heard. The words in this book are mine. Now that they're in print, I will not talk to anyone about these things ever again other than Zoe and Holly. They have both grown into two truly amazing young women and I'm very proud of them both.

When I began writing this book, I could feel myself reverting back to a little girl. Sometimes, I still feel haunted and very vulnerable, as if the shadows of the past are chasing me. But then there's the other part of me that says, "Wait, hang on a minute Mrs!" I turn around and see my daughters and remember the good things in life and I see my dogs running towards me from one of the fields on the 15 acres of Freedom Farm. Each one running from their own dark past. And we sit together on the grass in the sunlight, enjoying each other's company, all of us having finally found someone they can trust. It really doesn't get much better than that.

EVERY DONATION MATTERS

We're very appreciative of every gift left to us, no matter how small or large. Now that lockdown has ended, we're looking to bring more dogs over from China later in 2021. Every donation we receive helps care for the dogs who already live at Freedom Farm and to fund the Darkness to Light Project. Flights, boarding, vet bills and food for our dogs are expensive and getting more so with each passing year, so a one-time donation, a monthly allowance or even a small percentage or a fixed percentage of your estate would mean a lot to us.

You can learn more about the work we do and make a onetime or regular donation here:

https://rushtondogrescue.co.uk/donate/

or visit us on

https://www.facebook.com/rushtonrescue

or

www.instagram.com/rushtondogrescue.

One-time only or regular donations may be tax deductible. Please consult https://www.gov.uk/donating-to-charity for more information.

You can also visit our charity shop at 79 Portland Road in Wyke Regis. The proceeds from every purchase go towards the care and feeding of the dogs at Freedom Farm and towards the Darkness to Light Project.

If you want to leave us a gift in your will, you can leave three main types of gifts:

You can leave a residuary gift – a percentage of your estate after your family and friends are provided for – or you can leave a fixed sum of money, known as pecuniary gift. Residuary gifts are particularly helpful as they usually maintain or increase their value over time.

You could leave a specific gift such as a piece of jewellery or art.

Sample wording for your will

If you do decide to leave a gift for us in your will, we recommend discussing it with a solicitor. It is important to do so in order to ensure that all legal requirements are met and that your will is valid, using the samples below as a guide:

'I give _____% of my residuary estate or £ _____ to Rushton Dog Rescue Freedom Farm Henley, Langport TA10 9BE registered charity number 1139999 for its charitable purposes and I further direct that the receipt of the Treasurer or other proper officer of Rushton Dog Rescue for the time being shall be a full and sufficient discharge for the said legacy.'

A properly drafted will can help reduce the amount of tax payable on your estate and increase the value of the assets that you pass on to your loved ones.

If you already have a will

If you decide to leave a gift for us in your will, you may not need to make a new one. Small changes to your will can be stated in a document called a codicil, which is read in conjunction with your will.

However, your solicitor will need our registered address and charity details, which are:

Rushton Dog Rescue
Freedom Farm
Henley
Langport
TA10 9BE
Registered Charity Number 1139999

We also have an Amazon wish list. We use all the items for the animals' upkeep and the cost is tax deductible for the gift-giver.

https://www.amazon.co.uk/hz/wishlist/ ls/37RI1SSR4H33/?ref_=lol_ov_le

Please do note that we receive a high volume of emails daily asking about adoptions. Although we aim to reply to everyone in a timely manner, with all that we have going on here, we simply cannot respond to every single one. Applying does not equal success. We want every dog to find people as equally special as they are!

ACKNOWLEDGEMENTS

To everybody who supported me during my journey, I am thankful. To everyone who supported the journey of the charity, we are all very thankful.

Coming Soon…

Further books in this series will delve deeper into the stories of Cindi's childhood and life and tales of Rushton Dog Rescue.

Lightning Source UK Ltd.
Milton Keynes UK
UKHW051846291121
394796UK00003B/5

9 781739 862909